THE

GREAT TREE

ON

BOSTON COMMON.

BY

J. C. WARREN, M.D.,

PRESIDENT OF THE BOSTON SOCIETY OF NATURAL HISTORY.

BOSTON:
PRINTED BY JOHN WILSON & SON,
22, School Street.
1855.

THE

GREAT TREE ON THE COMMON.

At a meeting of the Boston Society of Natural History some time since, the age of the large elm on Boston Common became accidentally a subject of discussion. On this discussion, it appeared there was some difference of opinion, which led the writer of these remarks to make inquiry into the facts, and endeavor to ascertain the age of the tree. This inquiry seems to be of no great importance at first view; but, independently of serving for the gratification of a proper curiosity, it may assist us in establishing the period of the duration of this valuable ornament to our country.

We propose, then, to notice this tree, not because it is a larger tree than any other in the country, nor because it is older or taller. The Aspinwall elm has a greater diameter; there have been a number of trees, cut down from time to time, which have been thought to have a greater age; and the elm on Pittsfield Common, as we are informed by Professor Holmes, is a hundred and fourteen feet before the first branch is given off: of course, it is taller. This tree is an object of interest, from the fact of its being placed in the centre of Boston Common, and thence having attracted the attention of every native Bostonian. It is also interesting for other reasons. It has not only escaped the blasts which have occasionally threatened to annihilate it, but the more alarming threats of destruction from a British army encamped around it suffering under the severity of a winter's exposure. Thanks are due from the present and succeeding generations to General Gage, the commander of that army, for having preserved this and other valuable trees in Boston from being employed in protecting his troops against the severity of the climate.

It was the frequent scene, and in some measure the instrument, of inflicting vengeance on those whom popular indignation, whether justly or not, thought proper to stigmatize and terrify by hanging or burning in effigy. The writer was witness, and in some degree an adverse actor, in a scene of this kind during the political riots of 1806. At a later period, for many months, it had to withstand the dangers from the little army encamped around it, destined to protect the town in the war of 1812. Many tumultuous scenes have endangered its existence on the annual recurrence of Election and Independence days, when there was no restraint in the public use of stimulants, which on those occasions so often drove men to madness, bloodshed, and all kinds of excesses. These circumstances will perhaps be thought sufficient to justify the attention we have bestowed on it.

A drawing has been introduced to give an idea of its present appearance to a succeeding generation. The map was inserted to show, that in 1722 this tree was represented as the largest tree in Boston: it is a diminished copy of the earliest plan of Boston, viz., that of Capt. John Bonner, published in 1722. This gentleman had previously sketched some portions of the wharves in the proximity of Long Wharf. The sketches, though valuable, included no part of Boston but the wharves already mentioned; and the plan of 1722 is undoubtedly the earliest complete one. The only copy of it which existed for many years within my knowledge was in the possession of Joseph Peirce, Esq., of which I obtained a fac-simile to be drawn by a lady of Boston nearly forty years ago. In 1835, Mr. George H. Smith reprinted Bonner's plan, which corresponds with mine, and proves the exactness of the drawing. The diminished map is an exact copy of Capt. Bonner's; some trees, too small for representation in a diminished view, only being omitted. The Great Tree, and two trees at the head of Park Street, are well represented in their proportion to co-existing trees and to each other.

This tree is an American Elm, belonging to a species admired and cultivated abroad for its gracefully pendent branches. It is known by the most ancient surviving inhabitants of Boston as THE GREAT TREE. Citizens, who were of advanced age in the youth of those who are now the oldest inhabitants, knew it equally as THE GREAT TREE.

The writer of this, having always lived in the vicinity of the Common, where it is situated, and for half a century within sight of it, has a distinct recollection of its appearance for about seventy years.

When he first knew it, it bore strong marks of decrepitude and approaching dissolution. There was a large orifice in the bark of its trunk, through which a boy, eight or nine years old, could creep into its cavity; and in a picture wrought in 1755 by Miss Hannah Otis, aunt of the late distinguished orator and statesman, Harrison G. Otis, the same orifice is also represented, — thus adding thirty years to its known period of decrepitude.

The interior of the trunk was rotten, and much of it had disappeared. The aperture was from two to three feet in length, and about a foot in breadth. For many years, it was neglected; but when, in process of time, the spirit of improvement extended to its part of the Common, the edges of the aperture were protected by a mixture of clay and other substances, and the exterior covered by canvas fastened around it. In consequence of these attentions, the parts have been regenerated; and the opening, so far as can be ascertained, filled and obliterated.* We presume the

* The same process is now in successful operation in two American elms remaining in Park Street. The bark on the side towards the street was torn off by the passage of carriages. To accomplish their recovery, the trees were first guarded by forming a sideway with raised stones; and the wound, having been seasonably protected by a covering, has gradually healed, and is now reduced to a third part of its original dimensions. The trees, in the mean time, have increased a quarter part in size.

trunk to be weakened; and, if the tree possessed all its original branches, there would be danger of its being overturned by the wind. To what extent the interior has been repaired, it is impossible to determine; but that a portion of the cavity may have been obliterated by the formation of new woody fibre, is demonstrable by a specimen which happens to present itself at the moment of writing this. A violent wind-storm, which occurred on Sunday, June 10, 1855, tore off a hollow branch of a tree in the Hospital grounds; by which it appeared that the edges of the aperture were coated with bark, and this bark was supported by new woody fibre which had lately been generated by the leaves, and was thus gradually closing up the cavity.

Standing alone (as it has done), and unprotected by trees or houses, it has frequently been attacked by storms, and large branches torn off. In the month of June, 1831, a violent storm partially separated four large limbs, and so far detached them that they rested on the ground. Mr. James A. Sutton, now Master Block Maker at the Navy Yard, Charlestown (then apprentice to Mr. Daniel Adams, Pump and Block Maker), informs me that he was sent with a party of apprentices and citizens to endeavor to reinstate the prostrate limbs in their natural situation. By judicious efforts, they succeeded in raising and bolting them together. The bolts are still visible, and afford the only indications of these limbs having been separated, as they appear now at the end of twenty-three years to be completely united.

The branches, however, are greatly diminished in number, especially on the south-east side, which has suffered most from storms; and their beautifully pendent character is diminished, so that they no longer sweep the surface of the ground. But, although worn by the storms of ages, it is still a magnificent object. No doubt its peculiar situation has contributed to its growth, preservation, and renovation; for it stands in a rich hollow, near a permanent pond of water situated a little higher than its roots. In 1844, it was measured by the distinguished botanists, George B. Emerson, Esq., and Professor Asa Gray (*vide* "A Report on the Trees and Shrubs growing naturally in Mass."); at which time its measurement was as follows: "At the ground, 23 ft. 6 in.; at three feet, 17 ft. 11 in.; and at five feet, 16 ft. 1 in." Mr. Chesbrough, City Engineer, having recently measured this tree at our request, gives the dimensions as it now stands, viz.: "Height, 72½ ft.; height of first branch from the ground, 16½ ft.; girth, one foot above the ground, 22½ ft.; girth, four feet above the ground, 17 ft.; average diameter of greatest extent of branches, 101 ft."

The age and origin of this tree are matters of much interest to Bostonians. In a map in my possession, published during the administration of Governor Burnett, beautifully engraved and having the date of 1729, the Great Tree stands, as now, insulated from other trees: near it is the Pond, the ancient springs of which are now aided by a noble fountain of Cochituate water. At a short distance westward is represented the Powder Magazine, placed on a small well-known eminence, which, during the siege of Boston, was the seat of a British fortification. In another plan of Boston still older, 1722, a copy of which accompanies this work, it is again found in the same situation, an insulated tree, comparatively of great size. From its conspicuous appearance on the plans, we infer that it might have been more than a hundred years old at that time; and, of course, that it took its origin previous to the establishment of Governor Winthrop in Boston in 1630, or of Mr. William Blackstone before that period.

Some persons have thought, and it has been stated

in the "Boston Commercial Gazette" of April 25, 1825, but on what authority is not mentioned, that the tree was planted in 1670 by Capt. Henchman, an officer who had distinguished himself in the Indian wars. Capt. H. was a member of the Ancient and Honorable Artillery Company, an ancestor of Governor Hancock; and the statement says, that he planted this tree to shelter the Company during their parades on the Common. Many years ago, a venerable man and particular friend of mine, whom I have always supposed to be the author of the published account, made the same statement in the presence of a number of gentlemen. I took occasion to inform him, that this was probably a mistake; and, being shown the old plans of Boston, he appeared to be convinced of his error, and never repeated the story within my knowledge, though I conversed with him on the subject afterwards. I presume that he had no authority, excepting a report emanating from a lady who was a near relation of a descendant of Captain Henchman. There appears to be no sufficient foundation for this belief: if there is any good authority for the report, either traditionary or recorded, I am thus far unable, after diligent inquiry, to satisfy myself or any one else of its authenticity. It would seem also highly improbable that Captain Henchman or our earlier ancestors should have planted a tree for shelter in a situation so remote as that of this tree formerly was.

In the two plans of Boston, 1722 and 1729, it is always represented as a great tree; *i. e.*, greater than any other tree co-existing on these plans. There were within the memory of living persons two or three other trees of extraordinary magnitude. Two of these stood at the head of Park Street (*vide* Map), in what is now the Carriage-way: they, however, were obviously not of so great size. These two trees are not to be confounded with the two now standing in Park Street already mentioned, and which are also spoken of hereafter. If, then, this tree was a great tree in 1729 and 1722, it could not have been planted in 1670; for this would allow only fifty-two years for its growth. Its size and other characters would have required more than double that time at the earliest period of its representation.

The two plans above mentioned afford an opportunity of comparing the growth of well-known existing trees with the other, though they are not perhaps of exactly the same species. The trees in the Little Mall, so called, were planted by Colonel Adino Paddock in 1770.* They are, of course, more than eighty years old; and these trees are not so large as the earliest recollections of the Great Tree by persons now living. The trees in the Great Mall were planted, as appears from the plans, between the years 1722 and 1729. Those of them which remain are about one hundred and thirty years old, but have not the size of the Great Tree at the period of its notice, on the earliest plan.

It may be objected, that the growth of the American elm is very rapid; and that the tree, if planted in 1670, as is believed by some, if it had attained five or six years before being transplanted, might, in a period of fifty-two years more, reach a size which would entitle it to a respectable representation on a map of Boston. In order to determine the probability of such a growth, I have examined elms on my own place in Brookline, whose ages were from ten to sixty years. The largest and oldest individual of these, planted in the year 1798, is six feet in circumference

* Two of the walks in Boston were formerly designated by the names, "Great Mall" and "Little Mall." The "Great Mall" borders the eastern edge of the Common; and the "Little Mall," the eastern edge of the Granary Burying-ground. The last named was planted with English elms by Col. Paddock; the other, about fifty years previously, with a mixture of elms and buttonwoods (*platanus occidentalis*). Mr. Paddock was a loyalist, left Boston in the year 1776, and settled in Nova Scotia, where his descendants live and flourish.

at four feet from the surface of the ground: a dozen others, of the same age, have not more than two-thirds of these dimensions. An account of an elm situated in Ware, in this State, has been published in the newspapers, which is said to be about fifty years old, and has obtained the circumference of about twelve feet at six feet from the ground; the boughs covering an area whose circumference is about one hundred and fifty feet. The statement, however, is not made with any authority, and the facts are mentioned rather too loosely to form a ground of any important deduction.

Having lived, as before intimated, on the edge of the Common for nearly fifty years, my life has been long enough to notice the growth of some of its American elms. President Quincy in 1824 planted two rows of elms in Park-street Mall. These trees, thirty years of age, average in circumference less than four feet, in diameter a foot and a third. In Park Street, a line of elms was planted some years before I came to live there. This plantation, as far I can ascertain, was made in consequence of a donation to the town of a sum intended to improve the Common and its vicinity by Gov. Hancock, Gov. Bowdoin, Thomas Russell, Esq., and others, probably (as the Hancock family think) about the year

1786. The two trees remaining of this line measure, one of them, 7 ft. 3 in.; the other, 6 ft. 4½ in., in circumference; and, though more than sixty years old, they have thus but little over two feet in diameter, and cannot be considered as great trees. The distinguished gentleman named above, President Quincy, has on his ancestral seat at Quincy two walks of these trees planted within his knowledge. One of these was set out in the year 1790, being of the girth usually attained by the upland elms when at the height of ten or twelve feet; in number they were about two hundred. Of these elms, at four feet from the ground, five of the largest are now, after a period of nearly sixty-five years, of the average girth of 5 ft. 8 in. Five of the smallest average in girth 4 ft. 2 in. In the second walk set out in 1812, at the same distance from the ground, four of the largest are in girth 3 ft. 10 in.; four of the smallest, 3 ft. 2 in.; the period being forty-three years.

We may conclude then, I think, that the growth between 1670 and 1722, a period of fifty-two years, could not have entitled the Great Tree, so called, to the conspicuous representation it has on Bonner's map.

The history of other aged elms might perhaps aid

us in elucidating the point in question. There is one which has attracted notice, whose age may be determined with apparent certainty: it is the Aspinwall elm in Brookline, near the former Smallpox Hospital. This was planted in 1656, and must, of course, have been three or four years old at the time of its transplantation, so that at the present time it is at least two hundred years old. Its appearance leads us to believe it may live at least a hundred years more;* and this we think a fair age to assign to the American elm situated in favorable circumstances, so far as we are acquainted with its history. Whence we conclude there is nothing improbable in the belief that the Elm on Boston Common is more than two hundred years old.

But, as it was certainly the Great Tree in 1729 and 1722, we may indulge the belief, that it sprang up previous to the settlement of Boston; that it cast its protecting shade over the heads of our earliest American ancestors; and that even the native inhabi-

* Since writing the above passage, I have examined this tree, and find that its annual foliage has been almost wholly devoured by the canker-worm, in common with many other trees in the low land of Brookline. It appears at this time like a frightful skeleton; and there is a question whether it will ever recover from the shock it has received. In its death, we shall have to deplore the loss of one of the finest natural ornaments of this part of the country.

tant of the soil enjoyed the protection of its wide-spreading branches.

This tree, therefore, we must venerate as a visible relic of the Indian Shawmut; for all its other native trees and groves have been long since prostrated; the frail and transient memorials of the Aborigines have vanished; even the hills of Trimountain cannot be distinguished; and this native noble elm remains to present a substantial association of the existing with the former ages of Boston.

The present active and intelligent Mayor of our city, Dr. J. V. C. Smith, has erected a handsome iron fence as a permanent protection to this valuable relic of the early days of the city, with the following inscription, viz.: —

"THE OLD ELM.

"This tree has been standing here for an unknown period. It is believed to have existed before the settlement of Boston, being full grown in 1722. Exhibited marks of old age in 1792, and was nearly destroyed by a storm in 1832. Protected by an iron enclosure in 1854.

"J. V. C. SMITH, Mayor."

NOTES.

A POETIC imagination might present striking pictures of the various scenes which have occurred in the vicinity of this tree, from the period when it was surrounded by the native sons of the soil to that which was exhibited when the Common shone with the brilliant armor of British troops in 1768 and 1775. Among the multitude of interesting occurrences which have distinguished the spot where it stands, one or two may be mentioned.

The earliest of these, drawn from "The History of Boston, by Samuel G. Drake, Esq.," is in the following language: — "1676, July 27. Another of the Nipmuck Sachems, called 'Sagamore John,' influenced about one hundred and sixty Indians to surrender at Boston. One among them, old Matoonas, he brought in by force, being 'bound with cords.' He was immediately condemned to death; for he was not only the father of him who was hung in Boston several years before, but he was charged with being the first to commit murder in Massachusetts Colony in this war. His betrayer, 'Sagamore John,' was desirous that he and his men might be the executioners; wherefore Matoonas was carried out into the Common, and being tied to a tree, they then shot him to death."

There is a curious history of a fatal duel, of which the ground near this Tree was the seat, on July 3d, 1728. Two young gentlemen of the most distinguished families in the town were supposed to have disputed for the possession of a young lady, whose name is now buried in forgetfulness. The principal actors in this affair were Mr. Benjamin Woodbridge, a descendant of the family whose name stands first among the graduates of Harvard College; the other was Mr. Henry Phillips, of a family not less distinguished; both of them were about twenty years old. The combat took place in the evening. The parties contended with rapiers; and Woodbridge, being thrust through the body, lived but a short time. His antagonist fled, and took refuge in a British ship of war in the harbor, which safely transported him to the English shores; where, however, he could not escape from his own recollections, and died soon after, a victim to despair. The monument of Benjamin Woodbridge is still to be seen in the Granary Burying-ground at a short distance from the gate on the south side. The story is told in a very interesting way by the distinguished author, "The Sexton of the Old School," who is also well known by the signature of Sigma, in the "Boston Evening Transcript" for April 25, 1851. A collection of the valuable researches of this author into a distinct volume would be an interesting and important acquisition.

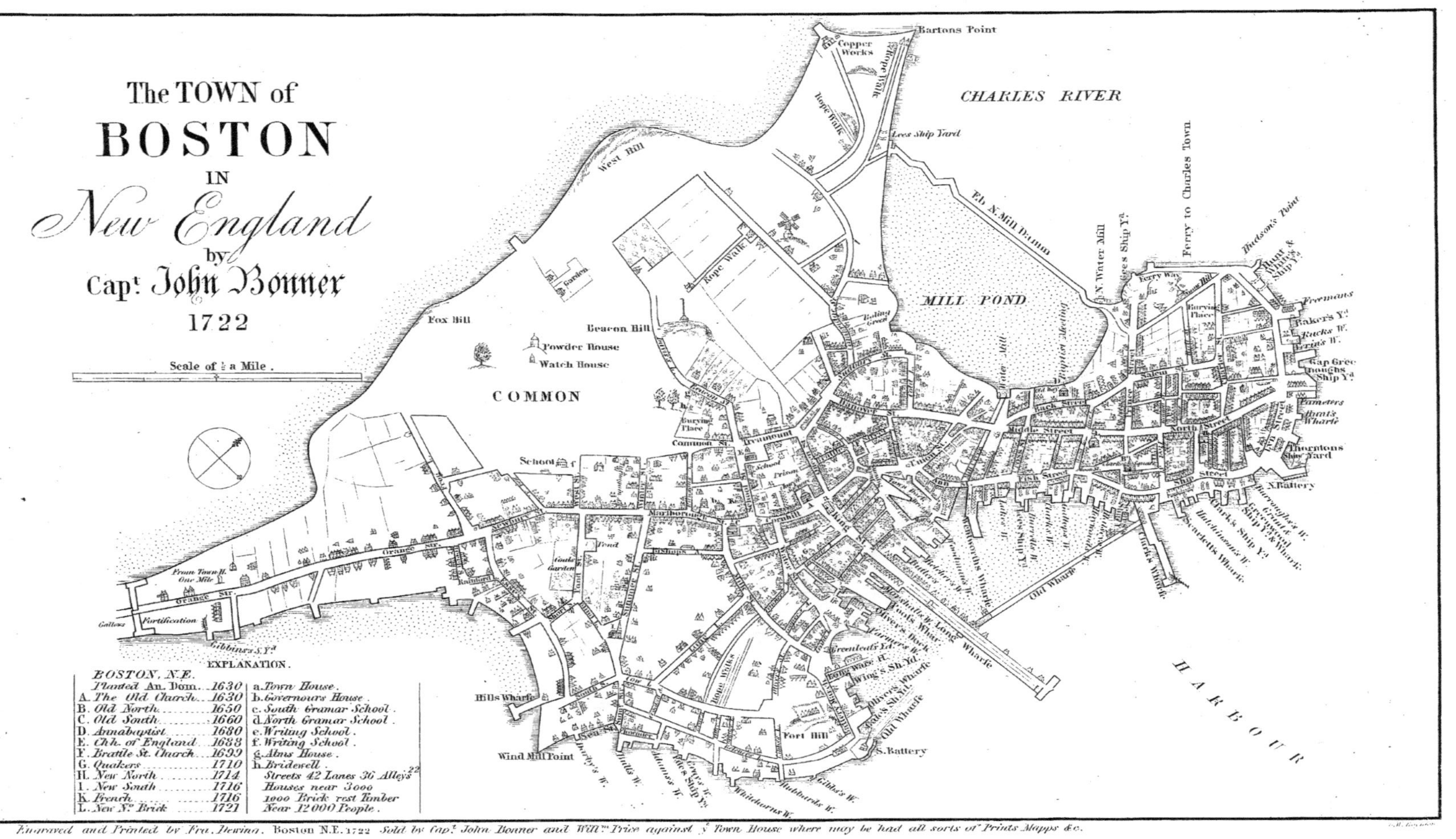

BOSTON, N.E.	
Planted An. Dom. ... 1630	a. Town House.
A. The Old Church ... 1630	b. Governours House.
B. Old North ... 1650	c. South Gramar School.
C. Old South ... 1660	d. North Gramar School.
D. Annabaptist ... 1680	e. Writing School.
E. Chh. of England ... 1688	f. Writing School.
F. Brattle St. Church ... 1699	g. Alms House.
G. Quakers ... 1710	h. Bridewell.
H. New North ... 1714	Streets 42 Lanes 36 Alleys 22
I. New South ... 1716	Houses near 3000
K. French ... 1716	1000 Brick rest Timber
L. New No. Brick ... 1721	Near 12000 People.

Engraved and Printed by Fra. Dewing. Boston N.E. 1722. Sold by Capt. John Bonner and Willm. Price against ye Town House where may be had all sorts of Prints Mapps &c.

www.ingramcontent.com/pod-product-compliance
Lightning Source LLC
LaVergne TN
LVHW011147110826
845150LV00008B/2558
* 9 7 8 1 4 1 8 1 9 3 2 1 8 *